**This book is to be returned on or before
the last date stamped below.**

D0120119

LIBREX

CONTENTS

snapping-turtle
guide

COPYRIGHT © 1999

ticktock PUBLISHING LTD UK

http://www.ticktock.co.uk

AWESOME POWER

An approaching hurricane brings with it torrential rain and high waves, which lash the coast. But it is when a hurricane first hits land that most of the damage and destruction take place, with whirling winds of over 120 km/h (75 mph).

HURRICANES
& TORNADOES

BY
NEIL MORRIS

WHAT IS A HURRICANE?

A hurricane is a large, very powerful storm with violent, whirling winds blowing at speeds of 120 km/h (75 mph) or more. Hurricanes, which meteorologists often call tropical cyclones, originate over warm oceans. They travel over the sea in the general direction of the wind, usually at about 20 km/h (12 mph), bringing with them heavy rain and stirring up high waves. When they reach land, hurricanes cause great damage and destruction. They blow down trees and houses, and the high sea waves and heavy rain often cause flooding along coastlines. Throughout history, hurricanes have been the cause of many terrible disasters. In recent times, scientists have learned a lot about how they form, but we are still powerless to stop them.

This photograph shows some of the damage caused to the city of Galveston, Texas, by Hurricane Alicia, in 1983. Twenty-one people were killed and it caused damage of $2 billion.

SHORELINE

A hurricane may measure more than 400 km (249 miles) across its spinning circle, and may last for many days before it eventually blows itself out. Ninety per cent of hurricane victims are claimed when the storm first comes ashore. Beneath the centre of the storm, the first tremendous winds and rain are followed by a period of calm as the eye of the hurricane passes overhead. Then the wind and rain hit again as the other half of the whirling storm passes over. As the hurricane moves across cooler land, it is no longer fed by warm rising air and starts to lose its power.

INSIDE A HURRICANE

When a hurricane forms, water vapour is picked up from the sea and makes thick walls of cloud. As the warm water vapour and air rise, they start to spin in an upward spiral. More warm, moist air rushes in underneath the rising air and the spinning air builds up to form a hurricane. The violent winds spin around a calm, cloud-free area of very low pressure, called the 'eye' of the hurricane.

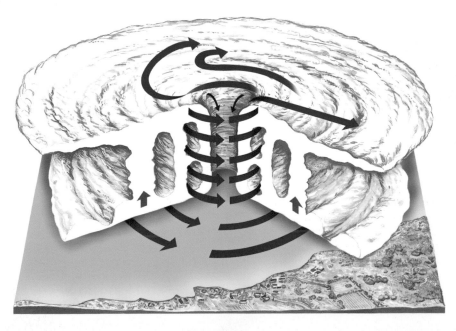

NAMING THE HURRICANE

Hurricanes are given names to identify them and to avoid confusion when there is more than one storm at the same time. The World Meteorological Organization chooses the names, which start from A each year and alternate between male and female names. In 1998, for example, the Atlantic hurricane names were Alex, Bonnie, Charley, Danielle, Earl, and so on. This infrared satellite photograph shows Hurricane Fran over the Caribbean in 1996. Fran's winds reached 190 km/h (118 mph) and the storm caused the deaths of 34 people.

This photograph clearly shows the calm eye in the middle of a hurricane, with thick white clouds whirling around it. At the top of the storm, dry, colder air from above is sucked down into the eye, which often measures about 30 km (19 miles) across.

WHERE IN THE WORLD?

ATLANTIC HURRICANES

The southeast corner of the United States is used to hurricanes. In September 1998, Hurricane Georges caused great flooding to the low-lying islands of the Florida Keys. More than 150 homes were completely destroyed by the storm, which had already killed more than 500 people on several Caribbean islands.

Hurricanes start in bands just north and south of the Equator called the tropics: the Tropic of Cancer north of the Equator, and the Tropic of Capricorn to the south. These are the hottest parts of the Earth, and so their oceans have very warm water. Oceans with a temperature above 27°C (81°F) produce the warm, moist vapour needed for a hurricane to form. When severe tropical storms occur in the western Pacific Ocean, they are known as typhoons, and in the Indian Ocean they are called cyclones.

TROPIC OF CANCER

EQUATOR

TROPIC OF CAPRICORN

PACIFIC TYPHOONS

High waves and storms were a common theme for Japanese artists, many of whom had probably experienced Pacific typhoons. Ando Hiroshige (1797-1858), a famous Japanese painter and printmaker, created many landscapes and seascapes, including this picture of wind-blown waves.

STORM CLOUDS

Long, low storm clouds gather over the sea. Storms occur when masses of warm and cold air meet. The air masses do not mix easily together and cause winds, while clouds form along the edge, which is called a front. Not all tropical storms, however, turn into hurricanes.

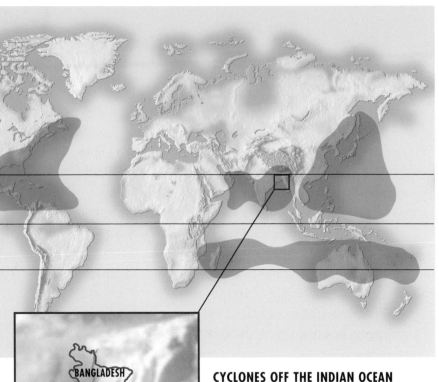

HURRICANE ZONES

The world's hurricane zones sit on the imaginary lines of the Tropics of Cancer and Capricorn and stretch across parts of the Atlantic, Pacific and Indian Oceans. Hurricanes usually travel westwards, pushed along by the trade winds. They then turn away from the Equator and pick up speed as they are affected by the Earth's spin. In the northern hemisphere, hurricanes always spin in an anticlockwise direction. Many hurricanes turn east when they reach cooler land or sea.

BANGLADESH

INDIA

Path of cyclones

CYCLONES OFF THE INDIAN OCEAN

This coastal region of Bangladesh lies directly in the path of many cyclones. The flat land of the Ganges delta is easily flooded, both by the sea and by the many channels of the river overflowing their banks. On 12 November 1970, a ferocious cyclone hit Bangladesh (which was then called East Pakistan). It caused a storm surge 15 metres (49 ft) high, and many of the islands of the delta were submerged. Up to 500,000 people were killed by the disastrous effects of the cyclone.

STORM SURGE

Hurricanes whip up the sea beneath them and make huge waves. At the centre of the storm, the low-pressure eye of the hurricane pulls up a dome of water up to eight metres (26 ft) high. As the whole swirling storm moves towards land, it pushes the large waves of a storm surge ahead of it. The surge eventually produces flooding on land, and in low-lying coastal areas these floods often cause more damage than the hurricane's winds.

ATLANTIC HURRICANES

AID RELIEF

Not only did people lose their homes to Hurricane Mitch, many also lost their livelihoods. Crops were destroyed, water became contaminated. Many of the world's richer countries and relief organizations gave money and supplies to Honduras and Nicaragua to help them survive the damage caused by Hurricane Mitch. Some of the devastated areas were very difficult to reach, and victims had to wait a long time before help reached them.

The Atlantic hurricane season runs from June to November, but the most violent storms usually occur in August and September.
This is when the ocean's waters are at their warmest. There are usually about six hurricanes every year, but sometimes there can be many more. In 1995, for example, 19 hurricanes were recorded. Most originate in the north Atlantic Ocean and then pass through the Caribbean Sea and the Gulf of Mexico, before turning towards mainland USA. In 1998, two devastating hurricanes struck one after the other. During September Hurricane Georges hit the Caribbean Islands and Florida. Then just four weeks later, Hurricane Mitch battered Central America.

The worst devastation caused by Hurricane Andrew lay in a band 30 km (19 miles) wide, including the entire town of Homestead.

HURRICANE ANDREW

In August 1992, this powerful category-4 hurricane passed over the Bahamas and Florida, before moving into the Gulf of Mexico and heading for Louisiana. It was travelling at 40 km/h (25 mph) with winds approaching 250 km/h (155 mph). There was plenty of advance warning, and millions of people were evacuated, but still 54 were killed. Hurricane Andrew caused $25 billion of damage, and on its way it also destroyed many of the instruments at the US National Hurricane Center near Miami.

AFTER HURRICANE MITCH

Hurricane Mitch began as a Caribbean tropical storm on 22 October 1998. Five days later it had reached wind speeds of 300 km/h (186 mph) and hit land in Honduras. Over the next few days thousands of people were killed and more than 200,000 people lost their homes. Floods from rivers and the sea soon covered over half the country's land and three-quarters of farming land was destroyed. The Honduran capital, Tegucigalpa, was completely ruined. A further 2,000 were killed in Nicaragua, with more victims in Guatemala and El Salvador.

INTENSITY SCALE

Herbert Saffir, an American engineer, gave his name to the Saffir-Simpson scale of hurricane intensity. The scale ranges from 1 to 5, with category-5 hurricanes, such as Mitch in 1998, causing catastrophic damage.

HURRICANE CATEGORY	WIND SPEED - KM/H (MPH)	DAMAGE
1	120-153 (75-95)	Minimal
2	154-177 (96-110)	Moderate
3	178-209 (111-130)	Extensive
4	210-249 (131-155)	Extreme
5	250+ (155+)	Catastrophic

HURAKAN

According to Mayan legend, Hurakan, the ancient god of winds and storms, dwelt in the mists above the great flood that covered the Earth. Hurakan kept repeating the word 'earth' until the solid world rose above the seas. When the gods became angry with the early human beings, Hurakan punished them with storms. It is said that Spanish explorers named severe storms after the Mayan god, and the word 'hurricane' comes from the Spanish word 'huracán'.

HONDURAS, 1998
SURVIVING MITCH

Laura Arriola lived in the village of Barra de Aguán, near the mouth of the Aguán river in Honduras. Her house was a distance from the sea and the river, but when Hurricane Mitch struck, the sea and river merged in a flood. Laura's house was swept away, and her husband and three children were drowned. But she managed to cling to some floating palm branches as she was carried out to sea, and then she made herself a small raft out of tree roots and driftwood. She found floating fruit and coconuts, and survived in this way for six days before being spotted by a ship and rescued. By then she was 120 km (75 miles) from her home.

THE PACIFIC ISLANDS

The thousands of islands facing the Pacific Ocean to the east and the South China Sea to the west are particularly at risk. They experience typhoons from June to December, corresponding with the region's rainy season. In the Philippines, in 1984, two major typhoons sank 11 ships and caused more than 1,600 deaths.

Hurricanes and typhoons have been used as a theme in a variety of Hollywood disaster movies. This 1940s film, Typhoon, starred Dorothy Lamour and Robert Preston. Earlier, Lamour also starred in Hurricane, set in the South Pacific.

Causeway Bay harbour in Hong Kong acts as a typhoon shelter for shipping. Whenever storms are predicted, it becomes a floating town, with junks, sampans and motor launches all moored for safety.

BIG WINDS OF THE PACIFIC

Every year on average, there are 11 tropical cyclones in the north-west Pacific Ocean. In this part of the world these storms are called typhoons, from the Chinese 'tai fung', which means 'big wind'. These storms usually occur between the summer and autumn months of June and November and, travelling westwards, threaten the coasts of Japan and China. Many cross the Philippines and pass through the South China Sea. In the southern Pacific, below the Equator, there may be four cyclones threatening the Pacific islands, New Guinea and Australia, where they are sometimes known as 'willy-willies', from an old Aboriginal word. These southern cyclones are most common later in the year, between December and March.

TYPHOEUS

In Greek mythology, Typhoeus or Typhon was son of Tartarus and Gaia. As shown in this ancient Greek sculpture, he was a monster with many heads, a man's body and a coiled snake's tail. The king of the gods, Zeus, fought a great battle with Typhoeus and finally buried him under Mount Etna. According to legend, he is the source of storm winds that cause devastation and shipwreck. The Greek word 'tuphon', meaning whirlwind, comes from this legend, another possible source for the English word 'typhoon'.

Comment les hommes du giant haan qui eftoiencet liste puissoit la aire deleurs ennemis.

KUBLAI KHAN

By 1279 Kublai Khan (1216-94), the grandson of Ghengis Khan, had conquered China and made it part of the great Mongol Empire. Two years later, he sent two large fleets of ships to invade the Japanese island of Kyushu, probably thinking this would be an easier task. But his ships were caught in a typhoon, and most of the 150,000 men were drowned or, if they were lucky enough to survive the typhoon, slaughtered by waiting Japanese troops.

THE PACIFIC OCEAN, 1902
FROM CONRAD'S *TYPHOON*

British novelist, Joseph Conrad (1857-1924) based his story on a voyage bound for the Indonesian island of Java, and on the character of his real-life captain, John MacWhirr.
Nobody – not even Captain MacWhirr, who alone on deck had caught sight of a white line of foam coming on at such a height that he couldn't believe his eyes – nobody was to know the steepness of the sea and the awful depth of the hollow the hurricane had scooped out behind the running wall of water. It raced to meet the ship, and, with a pause, as of girding the loins, the Nan-Shan lifted her bows and leaped...She dipped into the hollow straight down, as if going over the edge of the world. The engine-room toppled forward menacingly, like the inside of a tower nodding in an earthquake...At last she rose, staggering, as if she had to lift a mountain with her bows. 'Another one like this, and that's the last of her,' cried the chief.

9

THE INDIAN OCEAN

STUDYING STORMS

Captain Henry Piddington (1797-1858), a British sailor stationed in India, spent many years collecting information on ships caught in severe storms in the Indian Ocean. In his *Sailor's Hornbook for the Laws of Storms in All Parts of the World*, published in 1855, he called these storms cyclones, from the Greek word for the coil of a snake. Piddington also noted that a ship called the *Charles Heddles* whirled clockwise for nearly a week in a tropical storm off the coast of Mauritius.

In the northern Indian Ocean, there can be up to six cyclones a year. Most of these cyclones happen in October, at the end of the monsoon season, when warm winds blow right across the ocean towards India, carrying a huge amount of water vapour. South of the Equator, cyclones happen later, around December time. On average there are about eight of these each year, half of which move southwards towards Madagascar and the coast of Africa.

FLOOD BARRIER

In Bangladesh, most flood barriers have to be built by hand. A major Flood Action Plan, started in 1992, is attempting to change the course of rivers and raise existing embankments. The country's capital city, Dhaka, is on a low-lying site on the Buriganga, one of the medium-sized rivers of the Ganges delta. The city, with a population of more than 5 million, is very prone to flooding.

RÉUNION

The volcanic island of Réunion, in the south-west Indian Ocean, sometimes suffers great rainfall from cyclones. In 1966, Cyclone Denise caused 182.5 cm (72 inches) of rain to fall in one day. Then in 1980, Cyclone Hyacinthe dropped 567.8 cm (224 inches) over a 10-day period. The economy of this beautiful island is based on sugar, which is grown on nearly three-quarters of the cultivated land. Flooding causes great damage both physically and economically.

WAITING FOR FOOD

Relief agencies regularly set up emergency centres in Bangladesh, where people wait desperately for food. The military are often brought in to help distribute the food as quickly and fairly as possible.

FLOODED OUT

Almost every year thousands of people are made homeless by the many floods in Bangladesh, which are caused, or made worse, by cyclones.

Most of the 120 million Bangladeshis are farmers struggling to grow rice, fruit, jute and tea on small plots of land. Crops are often ruined by flooding as a result of cyclones, and then people are in desperate need of emergency food and shelter. A cyclone in 1991 affected up to 10 million Bangladeshis. In 1998, three-quarters of the country was flooded, claiming at least 500 lives and leaving 25 million people homeless.

This 19th-century picture shows the inhabitants of Mayotte, one of the Comoro Islands in the Indian Ocean, in a state of panic as a cyclone approaches.

BANGLADESH, 1970

LOCAL NEWSPAPER REPORTS ON THE DEVASTATION OF A CYCLONE

The small number of survivors are without food. I saw about 800 bodies lying on both sides of the dam badly damaged by the tidal wave. I saw at least 3,000 bodies littered along the road. Survivors wandered like mad people, crying out the names of their dead. There were 5,000 bodies in graves, 100 to 150 in each grave.

The tidal wave, as high as a two-storey building, has changed the map of the delta, sweeping away islands and making others. Whole communities have been destroyed and all their people and livestock killed.

BIGGEST STORMS

The most powerful storms are not always the most destructive. Reliable statistics of wind speeds, air-pressure readings, deaths and amount of damage caused by hurricanes and other storms have only been available in recent times. They show that damage depends on when and where a storm strikes, and how much warning could be given. In September 1935, a category-5 hurricane hit the Florida Keys and killed 408 people. Yet a month later another hurricane, which records suggest was probably less powerful, caused about 2,000 deaths in Haiti, Honduras and Jamaica.

FLORIDA, 1992
EYEWITNESS

I was on holiday with my family in Orlando, Florida, in August 1992. As Hurricane Andrew developed in the Atlantic and approached the Bahamas, local newspapers and TV reports became increasingly sure that it would hit Florida. By 23 August, everyone in the State was being warned to take action. They thought Andrew would strike Miami, 350 km (217 miles) south of Orlando, and told people to evacuate that area. Looking out of our Orlando apartment window, we saw that all the outside chairs, tables and sunshades had been sunk in the hotel swimming pool. Every movable item was put away or nailed down, and all available hotel rooms for miles around were taken by evacuees. The winds picked up strongly. Disney World attractions closed and there were tornado warnings on the 24-hour Weather Channel as Andrew moved across the State.

Neil Morris, the author

DEADLY MITCH
Hurricane Mitch (see page 7) set off a deadly chain of events in October 1998. Not only did it cause terrible flooding in Honduras, it also led to mudslides from the Casitas volcano in western Nicaragua. Mud washed down the mountain, carrying trees and killing at least 1,200 people. At the same time another nearby volcano, Cerro Negro, began spewing out lava and ash. This created a deadly combination of natural disasters.

HURRICANE CAMILLE
This category-5 hurricane hit the Mississippi coast in August 1969 and caused a storm surge over seven metres (23 ft) high. The storm killed 256 people, including 12 people on the third floor of an apartment block who ignored  warnings and were having a party to celebrate the coming of Camille. The tall building was flattened by the winds. Two days later, the spent hurricane dumped 76 cm (30 inches) of rain on central Virginia, causing mudslides and killing more people.

BOARDING UP

As Hurricane Andrew (see page 6) approached Florida in August 1992, the National Hurricane Center and other authorities advised and then ordered people to leave their homes and evacuate the area around Miami. More than a million people were involved, and very quickly every piece of plywood in every builders' yard had sold out, as people looked for materials to board up their doors and windows. Huge traffic jams built up on the roads leading from the coast. By the time Andrew hit land, at 4:52 on Monday, August 24, everyone was ready.

Even though Florida was prepared for Hurricane Andrew, still the unforeseen happened.

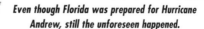

LABOR DAY

On Labor Day (2 September) in 1935, a category-5 hurricane hit Florida. It had a low pressure of just 892 millibars, the lowest recorded for an Atlantic hurricane. The storm drowned many of the islands of the Florida Keys, and its devastating winds snapped wooden and metal structures, including trees and steel railings.

TYPHOON TIP

One of the most powerful typhoons ever measured developed in the western Pacific Ocean in October 1979. When it was at its biggest, Tip covered an area over 2,000 km (1,243 miles) across, and was powerful enough to blow this freighter ashore near Tokyo. Fortunately for Japan and the Philippines, Tip spent most of its time and energy over the ocean.

DESTROYING DARWIN

This twisted metal memorial stands as a reminder of that Christmas Day disaster.

In 1974, the residents of Darwin in the Northern Territory of Australia had a Christmas they will never forget. Early on 20 December a tropical storm formed in the Arafura Sea, an extension of the south-western Pacific Ocean. Three days later the tropical storm had become a roaring cyclone, with winds whirling at over 200 km/h (124 mph). Cyclone Tracy, as it had been named, rounded Bathurst Island and hit the northern Australian port of Darwin four hours earlier than forecast at 1:30 a.m. on 25 December. The screeching winds blew everything away, making a roaring noise that survivors said sounded like a railway train coming out of a tunnel. Screaming residents ran into the dark streets, as their houses were torn from their foundations. Slowly the cyclone faded away, leaving the city of Darwin completely destroyed.

REBUILDING DARWIN

The Australian government set up a Reconstruction Commission immediately after Tracy struck. It was hoped to rebuild the capital of the Northern Territory within five years, something which was achieved in little more than three years. After the cyclone, there were only about 10,000 people left in the city. Now, Darwin is thriving once again and has a population of 81,000. Australian building regulations now state that houses in cyclone risk areas have to be specially protected against flying debris. In addition, their roofs have to be tied to the foundations. The authorities have taken steps to help people if such a cyclone should ever hit again, but they will always be at the mercy of natural forces.

DARWIN, 1974

BOB HEDDITCH, CAPTAIN OF A DARWIN FISHING BOAT

We put to sea on Christmas Eve at 19:30 hours and at midnight it hit us. The wind blew in our windows on the helm and tore off the back door. The waves crashed into the wheelhouse and I had to lie on the floor to steer. We had no steering by 02:00 hours, no lights and only the main engine to keep us heading into the gale. We lost both our anchors and I didn't have a clue where we were. We saw two boats send up distress signals, but there was nothing we could do. We limped back at 11:40 hours on the morning of Christmas Day. It was our engineer's first trip to sea. He disappeared when we docked. I think it was his last trip too!

TRAIL OF DESTRUCTION

About 10,000 homes, almost three-quarters of all the houses in Darwin, were destroyed by Cyclone Tracy. Sixty-five people were killed, the seriously injured numbered 145, and there were more than 500 minor injuries. Damage ran into hundreds of millions of Australian dollars. Tracy was a relatively small, but very severe cyclone. It measured 80 km (50 miles) across, with an eye of about 12 km (7 miles).

HOMELESS

As well as the winds, there was torrential rain: 255 mm (10 inches) fell in 12 hours overnight. About 25,000 people who had lost their homes had to be airlifted to other parts of the country, and by 29 December 10,000 people, including all the casualties and elderly people, had been evacuated.

CALM SEA

Today, Darwin is once again a calm, beautiful port. In 1974, as Cyclone Tracy was heading for the harbour, many ships tried to escape the approaching cyclone. Some were hurled onto rocks. Two navy ships sank in the harbour and one ran aground. Another ship was picked up and blown 200 metres (656 ft) inland. One observer said the harbour looked like a 'junkyard'.

WHAT IS A
TORNADO?

A tornado is a violent storm, much smaller than a hurricane, but with even stronger, whirling winds. The distinctive twisting whirlwind of a tornado hangs down from a dark thundercloud and touches the ground, like a spinning funnel. Some last for just a few seconds, while others go on for more than an hour. Most tornadoes move across the ground at speeds of 35 to 65 km/h (20 to 40 mph), and the damage they cause may be in a path over a kilometre (half a mile) wide and 100 km (62 miles) long. The funnel of a small tornado may be just 3 metres (10 ft) wide, while a big tornado might be a hundred times wider.

DAMAGE SCALE

T. Theodore Fujita, a professor of geophysical sciences at the University of Chicago, gave his name to the Fujita scale of tornado wind speeds and damage. The scale runs from 0 to 5, with category F-5 tornadoes causing incredible damage.

TORNADO CATEGORY	WIND SPEED - KM/H (MPH)	DAMAGE
F-0	up to 116 (72)	Light
F-1	117-180 (72-112)	Moderate
F-2	181-253 (113-157)	Considerable
F-3	254-332 (158-206)	Severe
F-4	333-419 (207-260)	Devastating
F-5	420+ (261+)	Incredible

Amateur enthusiasts, or 'storm chasers', sometimes have radar detectors in their cars to track and follow tornadoes. They keep a video camera with them at all times, so that they are ready to capture a promising storm on film. This dangerous hobby has provided scientists with useful pictures of many different kinds of tornadoes.

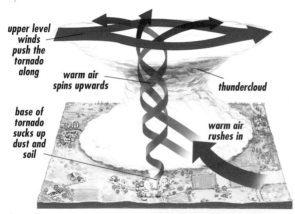

upper level winds push the tornado along

warm air spins upwards

thundercloud

base of tornado sucks up dust and soil

warm air rushes in

THE STRUCTURE OF A TORNADO

Like hurricanes, tornadoes form along fronts, where warm, moist air meets cool, dry air. A thundercloud forms, the warm air rises, and as more warm air rushes in to replace it, the air starts to spin. The spinning air forms a tornado, which, in the northern hemisphere, usually whirls anticlockwise. The tornado, with its thundercloud, is pushed along by winds higher up in the atmosphere. Sometimes several small tornadoes can form together from one thundercloud. Dust and soil are sucked up into the funnel, which whirls around a calm area of low pressure.

WATERSPOUT

**When tornadoes originate over
water, the water and spray
is sucked up into the clouds.**
These are called 'waterspouts' and,
although not usually as powerful as land
tornadoes, they can cause great damage
to shipping. The low pressure in the
funnel makes the surface of the sea
bulge upwards. Most waterspouts are
from six to 60 metres (20 to197 ft)
in diameter, and sometimes they
appear in pairs.

TORNADO ALLEY

Tornadoes happen all over the world, and are most common in North America, Europe, east Asia and Australia. In the United States, about 800 tornadoes are reported every year and around 70 people are killed. Waves of warm, moist air from the Gulf of Mexico often clash with cooler, dry winds from the northern states of Canada and the Rocky Mountains. This clash leads to many tornadoes forming along a wide stretch of country through the states of Texas, Oklahoma, Kansas and Nebraska, which has earned the region the nickname of 'tornado alley'. Most of the region's twisters occur in April, May and June, and they account for over a third of all US tornadoes. They usually occur during the afternoon or early evening, but there have been some night-time tornadoes. Florida is also often hit by tornadoes. It recently suffered when several deadly twisters hit Florida and Alabama in 1998.

TWISTER!

It is no good trying to simply outrun a tornado – it will almost certainly catch up with you. Anyone outside when a tornado approaches should try and move quickly away from the storm's path. If there is no time to escape the tornado's path, it is best to lie flat in the nearest ditch. Some houses in high-risk areas have an underground storm cellar for protection.

AREAS AFFECTED BY TORNADOES

THE ALLEY

An average of 125 tornadoes are reported in Texas every year, with over 50 in Oklahoma, 48 in Kansas and 38 in Nebraska. About 10 people are killed by twisters every year in Texas alone. This map shows how tornadoes are swept in by warm winds off the Gulf of Mexico.

TOTO

The National Severe Storms Laboratory is situated right in the middle of high-risk 'tornado alley' in Oklahoma. Scientists there have developed a barrel of instruments that can be dropped in a tornado's path to measure its temperature, air pressure, wind speed and direction. They call this the Totable Tornado Observatory — TOTO for short, after the name of the dog in *The Wonderful Wizard of Oz*. TOTO weighs 180 kg (397 lbs) and is transported on the back of a special pickup lorry.

TEXAN TWISTER

Texas suffers more tornadoes than any other state in the USA. On 11 May 1953, a single tornado hit Waco in central Texas, just 300 km (186 miles) from the coast of the Gulf of Mexico, killing 114 people. The worst US tragedy happened in 1925, when a group of tornadoes hit the states of Missouri, Illinois and Indiana, killing a total of 689 people.

DUST DEVIL

Sometimes when a tornado forms over a hot, dry region, it picks up a lot of flying dust and sand and is called a 'dust devil'. These dusty twisters seem to gather energy from the heat of the ground and can reach 300 metres (984 ft) up into the air. They are common in desert areas of the USA, Australia, India and Africa, including the Sahara Desert.

ACTION MOVIE

In the 1996 film *Twister*, **storm chasers spent much of their time trying to get inside tornadoes to learn all about them.** The film used amazing special effects to make the storms look convincing. On advertising posters for the film, tornadoes were called *'the dark side of nature'*.

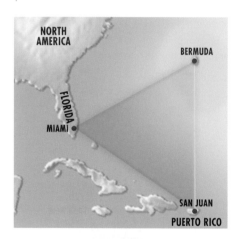

BERMUDA TRIANGLE

In the seas of the Atlantic Ocean between Bermuda, Florida and Puerto Rico, there is a mysterious area known as the Bermuda Triangle. Many ships and planes have disappeared here without trace. In 1945 a squadron of five US planes on a training mission vanished at the same time, and a search plane sent out to look for them also went missing. More than 50 ships are said to have disappeared in the region. One theory is that they were lost in storms, especially waterspouts, in that area.

In recent years there have been hundreds of cases of a phenomenon known as crop circles. A farmer suddenly discovers that some of the corn in his field has been flattened, usually in the form of a circle, making strange and interesting patterns. Some scientists have suggested that crop circles might have been caused by spiralling winds.

AMAZING WHIRLING WINDS

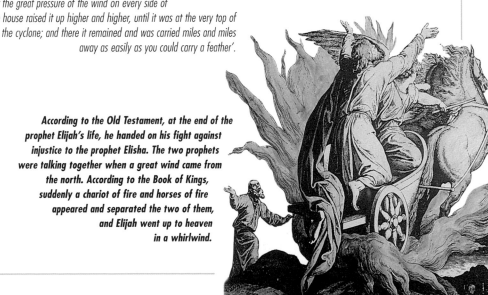

Hurricanes are easy to track, especially with today's scientific equipment, but tornadoes are often so unexpected and short-lived that we have suprisingly little information about them. Yet whirlwinds have existed throughout history; they have been mentioned in many accounts, including the Bible, and have formed part of many stories. One of the most famous whirlwinds formed the basis of *The Wonderful Wizard of Oz*. Whirling winds, tornadoes and waterspouts may also have been responsible for some of the world's great mysteries, which may never be solved.

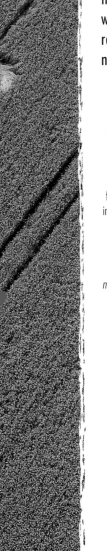

WIZARD OF OZ

L. Frank Baum's novel, *The Wonderful Wizard of Oz*, was published in 1900. It tells the story of Dorothy, who is swept away by a 'cyclone' from her aunt and uncle's farm in Kansas to the land of Oz. The book describes the Kansas farmhouse as '*standing at the centre of the whirlwind, where the north and south winds meet...In the middle of the cyclone the air is generally still, but the great pressure of the wind on every side of the house raised it up higher and higher, until it was at the very top of the cyclone; and there it remained and was carried miles and miles away as easily as you could carry a feather*'.

IT'S RAINING CATS AND DOGS!

Over the years there have been reports of many strange storms, including some carrying animals. These reports were probably related to tornadoes. There have been showers of fish, frogs and lizards. In 1978 in Norfolk, a flock of geese were picked up by the wind, and in 1997 in Nottinghamshire, pigs were seen flying through the air.

According to the Old Testament, at the end of the prophet Elijah's life, he handed on his fight against injustice to the prophet Elisha. The two prophets were talking together when a great wind came from the north. According to the Book of Kings, suddenly a chariot of fire and horses of fire appeared and separated the two of them, and Elijah went up to heaven in a whirlwind.

TORNADO SHELTER

Underground storm cellars give the best protection against tornadoes, but any basement offers some shelter. If the building has no basement, it is best to lie flat under a table or bed on the ground floor, away from any windows.

SAFETY PRECAUTIONS

In high-risk areas, the threat of hurricanes is always there. In some parts of the world, a television channel is devoted exclusively to forecasting the weather, but even with a warning, it is very difficult to know what precautions to take. As protection from the severe winds, homes should simply be secured and people evacuated as quickly as possible, before the storm strikes. Barriers can be built along the coast and rivers to help keep back destructive storm surges. In Rhode Island, USA, a hurricane killed more than 250 people in 1938. Today, the Fox Point Hurricane Dam on the Providence River can be closed during hurricanes and severe storms to protect the state capital, Providence, from flooding. Tornadoes are more difficult to predict and can arrive with very little warning.

These people are helping to build a high wall on the coast of Mindanao, the second largest island in the Philippines. After every disaster, the wall has to be repaired and built again. In wealthier parts of the world, higher, more permanent walls are built.

FLOOD BARRIERS

The best defence against storm surges and flooding are high sea walls. The 1,200 small coral islands of the Maldives, in the Indian Ocean, are especially at risk from flooding. Their highest point is just 3 metres (10 ft) above sea level, so the islanders have built special defences. This one helps protect the harbour at Malé, the country's capital.

STILT HOUSES

In coastal areas all over the world, houses are built on stilts to protect them from floods caused by tropical storms. This group of stilt houses is on an island in the Moluccas, Indonesia, where Pacific typhoons sometimes strike.

This storm cellar in the high-risk area of Arkansas was built above ground because of solid granite and limestone underneath the thin layer of soil. Reports state that it remained standing as fifteen residence blocks around it were destroyed.

EVACUATION ROUTE

Special road signs are needed to guide people to safety in a hurricane emergency without causing panic and confusion.

WEATHER WATCH

There are thousands of weather stations around the world, constantly measuring air temperature, air pressure and wind speed. More importantly for the forecasting of hurricanes and tornadoes, satellites are continuously watching and photographing the whole of our planet from positions high above the atmosphere. Their pictures quickly show where severe storms are developing. In addition, special planes and weather balloons observe and measure conditions in the upper part of the Earth's atmosphere. At the first signs of a tropical storm, the information is fed into computers, which use these details and also past information to enable scientists to predict the storm's course.

WILLIAM MCKINLEY

President William McKinley (1843-1901) said that he was more afraid of a hurricane than of the Spanish navy. During the Spanish-American War of 1898, President McKinley made the first effort to start a US hurricane service. Twenty-five years before, the first ever hurricane warning was issued in the United States, when members of the Signal Corps warned that a storm was approaching Connecticut.

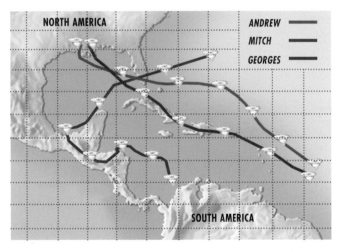

Satellite tracking can help detect the areas at risk by a hurricane. This map shows the position of various Caribbean hurricanes at 24-hour periods.

FLYING INTO A STORM

Special weather planes are sent to areas where storms are building, to gain the latest information. They are fitted with a long probe in their nose and are used to measure air conditions at different levels of the atmosphere. On board is special radar equipment to give a clear picture of cloud patterns. A reconnaissance flight may last up to 12 hours, during which time the plane may fly into the centre of the storm several times.

SATELLITE DETECTION

Meteorological satellites (or meteosats) beam picture signals to weather stations as they constantly orbit the Earth. These are checked by meteorologists to see if hurricanes are developing over the world's oceans. Four or five meteosats in the right positions can photograph the whole of the Earth's surface.

USING BAROMETERS

Weather forecasters use barometers to detect changes in air pressure. The barometer was invented by Evangelista Torricelli, an Italian physicist, in 1644 and measures the effect of air pressure on a metal chamber from which part of the air has been removed. Changes in air pressure make the chamber expand or contract, moving a needle on a dial. Modern barometers measure air pressure in millimetres or inches of mercury or in units called millibars. The atmospheric pressure at sea level averages 1,013 millibars, which equals 760 mm (30 inches) of mercury.

RECORDING PRESSURE

Scientists use a very accurate type of barometer called a barograph to record changes in atmospheric pressure. A barograph includes a pen that records the air pressure on a paper chart mounted on a rotating drum. Hurricanes and other storms build around areas of very low pressure, so barometers and barographs are very important instruments to weather forecasters.

FISHING

There is one possible benefit from severe storms. Fishermen have noticed that hurricanes stir up the depths of the sea. This disturbs the debris deep down, which is eaten by tiny creatures called plankton, which in turn encourage fish to feed. So without severe storms there would be fewer fish to catch. These fishermen are fishing off the coast of Venezuela.

BEAUFORT SCALE

The Beaufort scale of wind speeds was introduced in 1806 by Admiral Sir Francis Beaufort (1774-1857) of the British navy. Sir Francis surveyed and charted many of the world's seas, and he used the scale to describe wind effects on a fully rigged man-of-war sailing vessel. *Hurricanes are at the very top of the Beaufort scale of wind speeds.*

Force	Description	Wind speed-km/h(mph)
0	Calm	less than 1
1	Light air	1-5 (0.6-3)
2	Light breeze	6-11 (4-7)
3	Gentle breeze	12-19 (8-12)
4	Moderate wind	20-28 (13-17)
5	Fresh wind	29-38 (18-24)
6	Strong wind	39-49 (25-30)
7	Near gale	50-61 (31-38)
8	Gale	62-74 (39-46)
9	Severe gale	75-88 (47-55)
10	Storm	89-102 (56-63)
11	Severe storm	103-118 (64-73)
12	Hurricane	119+ (74+)

FORCE 1

THE WORLD'S WEATHER

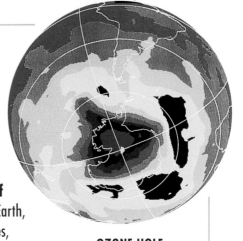

Extreme weather features such as hurricanes and tornadoes are just part of the overall climate of the Earth. When the Sun's rays reach the Earth, they warm the air; warm air is light and rises, while cold air is heavier and sinks. The movement of warm and cold air causes winds, which in turn sometimes cause storms. In the past century, the Earth's temperatures are gradually rising - 1995 was reported as being the hottest year on record. This global warming is being partly caused by 'greenhouse gases' in the atmosphere, which come mainly from some of the fuels we burn. This, along with other changes, could lead to higher global temperatures which, in turn, could result in coastal flooding, extreme winds and storms and other major climatic changes.

OZONE HOLE

Since the 1970s, satellite pictures have shown scientists that a gap appears each year in the atmosphere's protective layer of ozone. The first hole was seen over Antarctica, as shown in red on this satellite picture, and the second over the Arctic. The ozone has been attacked by chlorofluorocarbons (CFCs), gases that are used in aerosol sprays, refrigerators and in making plastics for fast-food packages. Changes such as this might have a great effect on the world's weather.

GLOBAL WINDS

There is a pattern to the world's winds. Their general direction is affected by the spinning of the Earth, which bends the flow of air towards the Equator westwards. These tropical trade winds blow in the regions where hurricanes form. As warm air rises at the Equator, it is replaced by cooler air from the cold polar regions. This maintains the balance of temperatures around the world.

COLD AIR

WARM AIR

EQUATOR

FORCE 6

FORCE 12

EL NIÑO

This oceanic and atmospheric phenomenon occurs when the warm waters of the Pacific Ocean flow eastwards towards the top part of South America, resulting in increased sea temperatures and climatic changes of varying severity. It is believed that El Niño is related to changes in air movements over the Pacific, which reverse the normal direction of the trade winds. El Niño is Spanish for 'the child'; the name refers to the baby Jesus Christ because the effect usually begins around Christmas time. It occurs about every three to seven years and can affect the world's climate for more than a year on each occasion. El Niño causes increased rainfall and storms in North and South America, including hurricanes and tornadoes and, at the other extreme, drought in Australia and Indonesia.

This damage was caused in 1997 by Hurricane Pauline, which hit the shanty towns of Acapulco, in Mexico, and was thought to be caused by the El Niño effect.

WARM CURRENTS

This computer-enhanced satellite image shows the warm currents of El Niño, coloured red, in the eastern Pacific Ocean off Central and South America. These currents warm the normally cool waters off the coast of Ecuador and Peru and bring torrential rain and flooding to the west coast of North and South America.

INCREASED STORMS

In the powerful El Niño of 1982/83, there was also an unusually large number of storms in California, but the 1997/98 effect is thought to have been one of the most intense. It caused a much greater number of tornadoes, freak storms and other disasters. There were violent outbreaks of twisters in California, and massive flooding in Peru.

This gold llama is an offering figure of the Incas. Around AD 1500 there was a mass sacrifice of 80 people by the Incas. Some scientists believe that this was a strong El Niño year, and that the sacrifices were carried out to try to appease angry storm gods.

SEARCHING FOR FISH

Pacific fish and the fishing industry suffer during El Niño years, especially off the coast of Peru. Peruvian fishermen have to sail much further from home to find a catch because small fish, such as anchovies, die or move away from warm waters in search of food. Warm water at the surface of the ocean blocks the deeper cold water, which is where many nutrients are found. Many larger fish, such as tuna, follow their main food supply. This has a big effect on the country, since Peru is traditionally one of the biggest fishing nations in the world, catching more than 11 million tonnes of fish per year.

WEIRD WEATHER

This small plane was hit by a tornado while it was on the ground in Florida. Meteorologists studying violent and freak storms are trying to work out how much El Niño affects the weather inland. Some believe that it has far more widespread effects than was previously thought. They have also discovered a similar effect that occurs in the Atlantic Ocean, and is known as the North Atlantic Oscillation, or NAO.

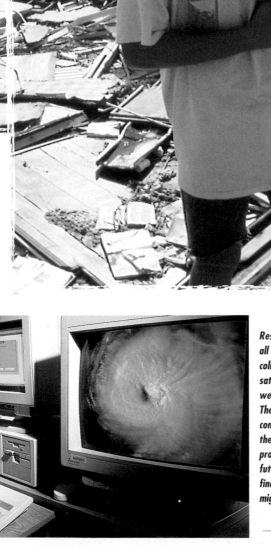

BUILDING A FUTURE

Amid the loss and destruction brought about by violent storms, there can still be a feeling of hope among the survivors. Communities are brought closer together by the wish to rebuild their homes and their lives. As a survivor of Hurricane Andrew said, *'We're alive and well. The rest is just stuff that can be replaced.'*

Research organizations all over the world collect data from satellites and weather stations. They use powerful computers to process the data and develop programmes to predict future storms, and find out what might happen.

LOOKING TO THE FUTURE

We will probably never be able to stop hurricanes and tornadoes, but perhaps we can learn to live with **severe storms and their effects.** Unfortunately, in many of the world's poorer countries – where a large number of these natural disasters occur – there are not the resources to cope with the phenomenal trail of devastation that results. Scientists and meteorologists are making studies all the time so that we can all improve our knowledge of these violent storms and what causes them. This will enable more accurate forecasts to be made, and provide useful information to enable more shelters and better defences to be built, especially in the world's biggest danger zones.

STUDYING EL NIÑO

There is a special programme to watch and measure the effects of El Niño and other weather phenomena. The TOPEX/Poseidon satellite monitors ocean circulations all over the globe, so that meteorologists can improve their predictions. Every 10 days the special satellite measures sea levels to an accuracy of within 13 cm (5 inches).

LOCAL STUDIES

Information from small weather stations all over the world will continue to be of great importance. They add to the data being produced by large centres and transmitted from space satellites, and they are particularly useful in forecasting local storms.

HELPING POOR REGIONS

In countries such as Bangladesh, aid workers are needed to help local people overcome the effects of disasters such as flooding caused by hurricanes and tornadoes. The world's richer nations must also help those in need to plan for the future, so that they are better prepared.

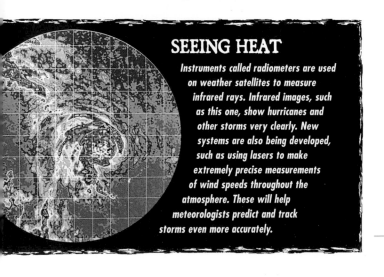

SEEING HEAT

Instruments called radiometers are used on weather satellites to measure infrared rays. Infrared images, such as this one, show hurricanes and other storms very clearly. New systems are also being developed, such as using lasers to make extremely precise measurements of wind speeds throughout the atmosphere. These will help meteorologists predict and track storms even more accurately.

DID YOU KNOW?

In the northern hemisphere, the winds are stronger at ground level on the right-hand side of a hurricane as it moves along. This is because the storm spins anticlockwise, and the spinning wind speed is added to the forward movement of the storm, called the storm speed. On the left-hand side the wind is blowing away from the direction of travel, making it less strong on the ground.

The names given to disastrous hurricanes that cause great damage and loss of life are dropped from future use. This is to avoid confusion and distress to relatives of victims. Since 1990 the names Andrew, Bob, Fran, Georges, Luis, Marilyn, Mitch, Opal and Roxanne have been dropped. By far the most catastrophic of these storms was Hurricane Mitch, which devastated Central America in 1998.

Witnesses have said that they have seen blue and orange lights at the centre of tornadoes. Scientists think that the lights might be caused by lightning within the tornado funnel. Many people have reported a high-pitched screaming noise as a tornado approached, and some have reported a strong smell like the ozone you smell at the seaside.

Scientists have tried to reduce the force of hurricanes by 'seeding' severe storm clouds with crystals of dry ice. The intention was to cause rainfall and release some of the energy of the hurricane. Unfortunately the experiments were unsuccessful.

In January 1974, a tornado in McComb, Mississippi, picked up and threw three school buses over a 2-metre (7 ft) high wall into woods. Fortunately the buses were empty at the time. In May 1990 near Plainfield, Illinois, a tornado hit a tractor-trailer. The tractor ended up more than 100 metres (328 ft) from the road, while the open trailer was found in a field a further 200 metres (656 ft) away.

ACKNOWLEDGEMENTS

We would like to thank: Graham Rich, Hazel Poole, Nicola Edwards and Elizabeth Wiggans for their assistance. Artwork by Peter Bull Art Studio.
Copyright © 1999 ticktock Publishing Ltd.
First published in Great Britain by ticktock Publishing Ltd., Century Place, Lamberts Road, Tunbridge Wells, Kent, Great Britain.
All rights reserved.
No part of this publication may be reproduced, stored in a retrieval system, or transmitted in any form or by any means electronic, mechanical, photocopying, recording or otherwise, without prior written permission of the copyright owner.
A CIP catalogue record for this book is available from the British Library. ISBN 1 86007 109 0 (paperback). 1 86007 121 X (hardback).

Picture research by Image Select. Printed in Belgium

Picture Credits: t = top, b = bottom, c = centre, l = left, r=right, OFC = outside front cover, OBC = outside back cover, IFC = inside front cover

Ancient Art & Architecture; 9tr, 21br. Ann Ronan @ Image Select; 10tl, 11b, 16tl, 23br, 24tl. Associated Press; 12br, 13br. Colorific!; 6bl & OBC, 8br,14/15b, 23bl, 30bl, 30/31 (main pic). Corbis; 7bl, 10bl, 21c,22tl, 31cl. e.t.archive; 4c, 9b, 28bl. FPG; 12/13b, 22/23bl. G Allen; 26/27b. Kobal; 20t. National Geographic; 12tr, 18cr. NHPA; 14br, 14/15t. National Met Library; 26cl. Oxford Scientific Films; OFC (main pic, SSEC/UW-Madison), OFC (inset pic), 28/29 (main pic), 28/29cb. Planet Earth; 16/17 (main pic) & 32, 27tr 28cl, 30/31cb. Popperfoto; 6/7t. Rex; 4tl, 10/11tl, 16cr,18tl, 29bc, 28tl, 31br, 31tr. Ronald Grant Arcive; IFC, 8bl. Science Photo Library; 2cl (Omikron), 2tl & OBC (Sam Pierson Jr), 2/3t (NASA), 3br (Hasler & Pierce, NASA), 6cr (NOAA), 20/21mp, 24/25 (main pic), 25cb. Spectrum Colour Library; 10bl, 14tl, 14cl. Still Pictures; 6tl, 8/9t, 12c, 22/23tr, 23cr, 26/27 (main pic). Telegraph Colour Library; 4b, 19br 21tr, 25cr. Tony Hobbs; 24br. Tony Stone; 12/13t, 18/19 (main pic).

Every effort has been made to trace the copyright holders and we apologize in advance for any unintentional omissions.
We would be pleased to insert the appropriate acknowledgement in any subsequent edition of this publication.

snapping-turtle guide

INDEX